Swimming and Diving

BY ALLAN MOREY

AMICUS HIGH INTEREST 🐟 AMICUS INK

Amicus High Interest and Amicus Ink are imprints of Amicus
P.O. Box 1329, Mankato, MN 56002
www.amicuspublishing.us

Library of Congress Cataloging-in-Publication Data
Morey, Allan.
 Swimming and diving / by Allan Morey.
    pages cm. – (Summer Olympic sports)
 Includes index.
 Summary: "Presents information about swimming and diving
in the Olympics including different types of swimming strokes,
different diving events, and synchronized swimming"– Provided
by publisher.
 ISBN 978-1-60753-809-7 (library binding)
 ISBN 978-1-60753-898-1 (ebook)
 ISBN 978-1-68152-050-6 (paperback)
 1. Swimming–Juvenile literature. 2. Diving–Juvenile literature.
 3. Olympics–Juvenile literature. I. Title.
 GV837.6.M67 2016
 797.2–dc23
                                    2014045801

Editor: Wendy Dieker
Series Designer: Kathleen Petelinsek
Book Designer: Aubrey Harper
Photo Researcher: Derek Brown

Photo Credits: Tim Tadder/Corbis cover; Christinne Muschi
/Reuters/Corbis 5; Elizabeth Kreutz/NewSport/Corbis 6;
Paul Riddle/VIEW/Corbis 9; Tim Wimborne/Reuters/Corbis
10; Chris Schmid Photography / Alamy 13; Chris Schmid /
Eyemage Media / Alamy 14; PCN Photography / Alamy
16-17; Catherine Ivill/AMA/Matthew Ashton/AMA Sports
Photo/AMA/Corbis 18; Chuck Myers/MCT via Getty Images
21; PCN/Corbis 22; Mark J. Terrill/AP/Corbis 25; Associated
Press 26-27; Lee Jin-man/AP/Corbis 29

Printed in Malaysia

HC 10 9 8 7 6 5 4 3 2 1
PB 10 9 8 7 6 5 4 3 2 1

Table of Contents

Going for the Gold

Splash! The swimmers dive off the blocks into the pool. It's a close race, but only one can be the winner. Every four years, the world's best swimmers and divers meet. They race. They dance. They leap and splash, all in hopes of winning a gold medal.

A swimming race starts! Who will win the gold medal?

Olympic superstar Michael Phelps dives into the pool for the 100m butterfly race in 2008.

Water sports have always been part of the Olympics. At first, only men competed. By 1912, both men and women were going for the gold in races and diving. Swimmers and divers are now part of **FINA**. This group makes the rules for all water sports. It also has races and events around the world. The best swimmers and divers go to the Olympics.

Swimming

Swimming has changed a lot over the years. The first Olympic races were held in lakes and rivers. Swimmers swam in cold water. They struggled against the waves. There were only four races. Today, we watch 34 races. And most races are held in warm indoor pools. The races have changed, but they are still exciting!

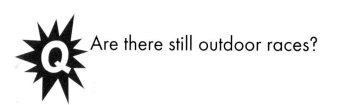 Are there still outdoor races?

Fans fill the Olympic aquatic center in London for the 2012 games.

 Yes! Watch the open water 10-kilometer marathon. These swimmers might battle wind and waves to win a medal.

Gold medalist Giaan Rooney from Australia does the backstroke.

Swimmers use four basic strokes. The fastest one is the front crawl. You'll also see the backstroke. It is like the front crawl, but swimmers race on their backs. The breaststroke and butterfly are the other two strokes. Swimmers bob up and down across the pool with these two front strokes.

There are two main races for each stroke. Swimmers race 100 meters (100m) or 200m. For the **freestyle races**, swimmers go other distances. The shortest race is one **lap**, or the 50m. One of the longest is the 1500m. That is 30 laps! **Medleys** are a mix of all the strokes. You'll see a different stroke every one or two laps.

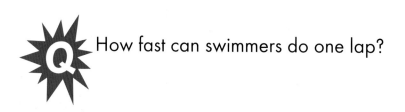

How fast can swimmers do one lap?

A backstroke lap starts by
pushing off the wall of the pool.

 In less than 30 seconds! In 2008, Cesar
Cielo Filho from Brazil set a 50m record.
He swam a lap in 21.3 seconds!

Gold medalist Rebecca Soni
swims the 200m butterfly
at the 2012 Olympics.

Q Who is the best swimmer ever?

The US swimmers are some of the best in the world. They have won more than 500 medals! The next best country is Australia. But they have won only 178 medals. Every four years, other swimmers try to beat the US swimmers. Not very many of them do.

 Most people say Michael Phelps is. This US swimmer has been to the Olympics four times and has won 22 medals.

Some of the most exciting races are the relays. This race is for a team of four swimmers. Each one takes a turn doing one or two laps. Here comes the first swimmer! The second one is ready to dive in. And he's off! The fastest team wins the gold medal.

A swimmer dives in for the next lap when his teammate touches the wall.

British platform diver Tom Daly slips into the water in the 2012 Olympics.

Diving

Divers don't just dive into the water. They leap, twist, and flip all before they hit the water. You will see two types of diving. Springboard divers use a bouncy board. It is 3 meters above the water. Platform divers leap from a stiff board high in the air. It is 10 meters high. That's as tall as a 3-story building!

Judges score divers on many things. They look at how divers take off from the board. They watch the flight. Are the movements smooth and correct? Last, they check the entry into the water. The smaller the splash, the better. In the **synchronized** events, judges score on how well the two divers match each other's moves.

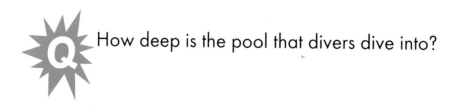

How deep is the pool that divers dive into?

These synchronized divers from Malaysia do the exact same dive.

The "diving pit" is 16.4 feet (5 m) deep.

Chinese diver Lin Yue pulls into a pike position as he flips off the platform.

Who is the best diver ever?

At the Summer Games, there are three rounds of diving. First is a **qualifying** round. Then come the **semi-finals**. The best divers move on to the final round. Men make six dives each round. Women do five. The scores from the dives are added up. The divers with the best scores win the gold medals!

 Many say Guo Jingjing from China. She won six medals from 2000 to 2008. Four of them are gold and two are silver.

Synchronized Swimming

What are the most popular sports at the Summer Games? Gymnastics and swimming. What do you get if you mix them together? You will get women's synchronized swimming. These swimmers leap and dive. They spin and twirl. They dance to music. This incredible sport became part of the Summer Olympics in 1984.

This team from China prepares
to do an underwater lift. Wow!

You will see **duet** and team events. For duets, two swimmers dance together. They try to match each other's moves as they swim. Teams have eight members. They do some fantastic dance moves in the water. Swimmers seem to dance on top of the water. They even toss each other into the air.

Lifts in the pool take awesome strength!

Swimming to Gold

Water sports are fun to watch. At the Olympics, the pool is a busy place. Hundreds of swimmers and divers compete. They meet every four years to race, dive, and dance. Who will take home the next gold medal? Keep an eye on the pool to find out!

The US swimming relay team members show off their gold medals in 2012.

Glossary

duet A group of two swimmers.

FINA In French, it is short for the Fédération Internationale de Natation, which means International Swimming Federation; this group makes the rules for international water sports.

freestyle race A swimming race where racers choose the stroke; most do the front crawl stroke.

lap One length of the pool, or 50 meters.

medley A swimming race that includes all four strokes in one race.

qualifying The first round of swimming or diving; the winners in a qualifying round move on to the next round.

semi-finals The second-to-last round in a swimming or diving competition; the winners in a semi-final round go to the final round.

synchronized Done together at the same time; synchronized diving and synchronized swimming are events at the Summer Olympics.

Read More

Gifford, Clive. *Swimming and Diving*. Mankato, Minn.: Amicus, 2012.

LeBoutillier, Nate. *Swimming*. Mankato, Minn.: Creative Education, 2012.

Hovde, Lynn and Nancy Speser. *Simply Synchro*. Quilcene, WA: Blue Horizons Publishing Company, 2013.

Websites

Olympic Swimming
www.olympic.org/swimming

Olympic Diving
www.olympic.org/diving

USA Synchronized Swimming
www.teamusa.org/USA-Synchronized-Swimming

Index

About the Author

Allan Morey was never an Olympic athlete, but he has always enjoyed sports, from playing basketball to going to baseball games and watching football on TV. His favorite summer sports are volleyball and disc golf. Morey writes books for children and lives in St. Paul, Minnesota, with his family and dog, Ty.